Car Safety

by Lisa M. Herrington

Content Consultant

Debra Holtzman, J.D., M.A.

Reading Consultant

Jeanne Clidas, Ph.D.
Reading Specialist

Children's Press®
An Imprint of Scholastic Inc.
New York Toronto London Auckland Sydney
Mexico City New Delhi Hong Kong
Danbury, Connecticut

Dear Parent/Educator:

It is very important that children learn how to be safe in and around cars. However, this is something they might need help with from a grown-up. If your child needs that help, we hope you will use this book as a springboard to a discussion about car safety with him or her. You can read the book together the first time, and talk about the different suggestions inside.

Library of Congress Cataloging-in-Publication Data
Herrington, Lisa M.
  Car safety / by Lisa M. Herrington.
    p. cm. — (Rookie read-about safety)
  Includes index.
  ISBN 978-0-531-28969-3 (library binding) — ISBN 978-0-531-29271-6 (pbk.)
  1. Automobiles—Safety appliances—Juvenile literature. 2. Traffic safety—Juvenile
literature. I. Title.
  TL159.5.H47 2012
  363.12'5—dc23   2012013373

Produced by Spooky Cheetah Press

Photographs © 2013: Alamy Images/BE&W agencja fotograficzna Sp. Z o.o: 15;
Media Bakery: 23 (DreamPictures), 7 (Dylan Ellis), 6 (Randy Faris); Shutterstock,
Inc.: 19 (Dmitry Morgan), cover (Lisa S.), 24 (Sandra Gligorijevic); Thinkstock: 28
(Barry Austin Photography), 4, 20 (Comstock), 12 (Creatas Images), 31 bottom left,
31 bottom right (iStockphoto), 8 (Stockbyte), 3 bottom, 31 top right (Zedcor Wholly
Owned/Getty Images), 3 top, 11, 27, 31 top left.

Table of Contents

On the Go

Vroom! Riding in a car can be fun! First you need to learn how to be safe in and around cars.

Kids under age 13 need to ride in the backseat. It is the safest place.

Buckle Up!

Little kids ride in a car seat that faces the back window until they are at least two years old. The seat is strapped into the car.

9

As kids get bigger, they move to a car seat that faces front. The type of seat is based on a child's age and size.

After a car seat, some kids still need a boost. They use booster seats. They ride in them until they are big enough to wear seat belts the right way.

Always wear your seat belt, no matter where you are sitting. Stay buckled until the car is stopped.

Shoulder belt should be snug across your shoulder—not under your arm or across your neck or face.

Lap belt should rest on the upper thighs—not across the stomach.

No Kidding

The driver needs to pay attention to the road. Do not bother the driver by fooling around in the backseat.

Never play with doors or windows.
Your hands can get caught in
power windows. Always keep your
hands and head inside the car.

19

Cars are not toys! Never play in or around them. Trunks are for storage, not for playing. You can get locked inside.

More Road Rules

Be safe outside the car, too. Exit and enter on the curb side only.

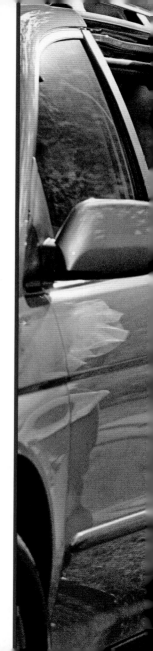

Hold a grown-up's hand when you cross the street. Watch out for cars. Before you cross, look left, then right, and then left again.

Always use crosswalks. A sign tells you when it is safe to cross the street.

Be careful in parking lots. Cars back up. Drivers might not see you. Follow these safety rules to make car travel fun!

Try It! Look through the book. Find the photo that shows how *you* ride in the car.

I Can Be Safe!

- Always wear your seat belt.

- Ride in the backseat.

- Do not distract the driver.

- Do not play in or around cars.

- Hold hands with a grown-up when crossing the street.

- Be careful in parking lots.

Words You Know

car

car seat

crosswalk

seat belt

Index

Facts for Now

Visit this Scholastic Web site for more information on car safety:
www.factsfornow.scholastic.com
Enter the keyword **Car**

About the Author

Lisa M. Herrington writes print and digital materials for kids, teachers, and parents. She lives in Connecticut with her husband and daughter. She hopes all kids stay safe!